Better Homes and Gardens.

Low-Fat Main Dishes

Easy Everyday Recipe Library

BETTER HOMES AND GARDENS® BOOKS
Des Moines, Iowa

EASY EVERYDAY RECIPE LIBRARY

Better Homes and Gardens® Books, An imprint of Meredith® Books
Published for Creative World Enterprises LP, West Chester, Pennsylvania
www.creativeworldcooking.com

Low-Fat Main Dishes
Project Editors: Spectrum Communication Services, Inc.
Project Designers: Seif Visual Communications
Copy Chief: Catherine Hamrick
Copy and Production Editor: Terri Fredrickson
Contributing Proofreaders: Kathy Eastman, Susan J. Kling
Electronic Production Coordinator: Paula Forest
Editorial and Design Assistants: Judy Bailey, Mary Lee Gavin, Karen Schirm
Test Kitchen Director: Lynn Blanchard
Production Director: Douglas M. Johnston
Production Managers: Pam Kvitne, Marjorie J. Schenkelberg

Meredith® Books
Editor in Chief: James D. Blume
Design Director: Matt Strelecki
Managing Editor: Gregory H. Kayko

Director, Sales & Marketing, Retail: Michael A. Peterson
Director, Sales & Marketing, Special Markets: Rita McMullen
Director, Sales & Marketing, Home & Garden Center Channel: Ray Wolf
Director, Operations: George A. Susral

Vice President, General Manager: Jamie L. Martin

Better Homes and Gardens® **Magazine**
Editor in Chief: Jean LemMon
Executive Food Editor: Nancy Byal

Meredith Publishing Group
President, Publishing Group: Christopher M. Little
Vice President, Consumer Marketing & Development: Hal Oringer

Meredith Corporation
Chairman and Chief Executive Officer: William T. Kerr

Chairman of the Executive Committee: E. T. Meredith III

Creative World Enterprises LP
Publisher: Richard J. Petrone
Design Consultants to Creative World Enterprises: Coastline Studios, Orlando, Florida

All of us at Better Homes and Gardens® Books are dedicated to providing you with the information and ideas you need to create delicious foods. We welcome your comments and suggestions. Write to us at: Better Homes and Gardens Books, Cookbook Editorial Department, 1716 Locust St., Des Moines, Iowa 50309-3023.

Our seal assures you that every recipe in *Low-Fat Main Dishes* has been tested in the Better Homes and Gardens® Test Kitchen. This means that each recipe is practical and reliable, and meets our high standards of taste appeal. We guarantee your satisfaction with this book for as long as you own it.

Cover photo: Peppered Pork & Apricot Salad
(see recipe, page 19)

Cooking family-pleasing meals night after night challenges the best of cooks. And, for those who aim to serve low-fat and great-tasting dishes, the task becomes even more difficult. But, with the aid of *Low-Fat Main Dishes,* high-flavor, low-fat cooking is easy.

In this collection, you'll find an innovative selection of anyday entrées—including vegetarian specialties—that boast simplicity and full flavors. Once your family samples these enticing recipes, they'll be convinced low fat never tasted better!

CONTENTS

Meat 6

Poultry 22

Fish & Seafood .32

Meatless 41

Index 46

Garlic-Sage-Marinated Beef Pot Roast

Red wine, tomato paste, and garlic give this fork-tender roast a robust, well-rounded flavor.

1	2- to 2½-pound boneless beef chuck pot roast
¾	cup dry red wine or tomato juice
2	tablespoons tomato paste
1	tablespoon snipped fresh sage or ½ teaspoon ground sage
10	cloves garlic, halved
2	teaspoons instant beef bouillon granules
¼	teaspoon pepper
1	tablespoon cooking oil
1¼	pounds tiny new potatoes or 4 medium potatoes
4	medium carrots, cut into 2-inch pieces
2	small onions, cut into wedges
2	stalks celery, bias-sliced into 1-inch pieces
½	cup cold water
¼	cup all-purpose flour
	Salt
	Pepper

Trim fat from meat. Place meat in a plastic bag and set the bag into a shallow dish. For marinade, in a small bowl combine the wine or tomato juice, tomato paste, sage, garlic, bouillon granules, and ¼ teaspoon pepper. Pour over meat; seal bag. Marinate in the refrigerator for 6 to 24 hours, turning bag occasionally. Drain meat, reserving marinade.

In a Dutch oven brown meat on both sides in hot oil. Drain fat. Pour marinade over meat. Bring to boiling; reduce heat. Cover and simmer for 1 hour.

Remove a narrow strip of peel from around center of each new potato. (Or, peel and quarter each medium potato.) Add potatoes, carrots, onions, and celery to meat. Cover and simmer for 45 to 60 minutes or till meat and vegetables are tender, adding some water if necessary. Transfer meat and vegetables to a platter. Cover and keep warm while preparing gravy.

For gravy, measure pan juices; skim fat. If necessary, add water to equal 1¾ cups liquid; return to Dutch oven. Combine the ½ cup water and flour; stir into juices. Cook and stir till thickened and bubbly. Cook and stir for 1 minute more. Season to taste with salt and pepper. Serve gravy with meat and vegetables. Makes 8 servings.

Nutrition information per serving: 321 calories, 29 g protein, 28 g carbohydrate, 8 g fat (3 g saturated), 78 mg cholesterol, 345 mg sodium.

Marinated Steak Fajitas

Fajitas are the rage in Mexican restaurants but you can easily make them at home. Top them with fat-free dairy sour cream, chopped tomato, and fresh cilantro, if you like.

1   pound beef flank steak
3   tablespoons chili sauce
2   tablespoons water
1   tablespoon Worcestershire sauce
1   teaspoon dried oregano, crushed
½   teaspoon chili powder
⅛   teaspoon garlic powder
⅛   teaspoon black pepper
10 7-inch flour tortillas
    Nonstick spray coating
2   small red, yellow, or green sweet
        peppers, cut into thin bite-size
        strips
1   small onion, cut into thin wedges

Trim fat from meat. Thinly slice meat across the grain into bite-size strips. Place meat in a plastic bag and set bag into a shallow dish. For marinade, in a small bowl stir together chili sauce, water, Worcestershire sauce, oregano, chili powder, garlic powder, and black pepper. Pour over meat; seal bag. Marinate in the refrigerator for 4 to 24 hours, turning the bag occasionally.

Wrap tortillas in foil and bake in a 350° oven about 10 minutes or till warm. [Or, just before serving, microwave tortillas, covered, on 100% power (high) about 1 minute or till warm.]

Spray an unheated large nonstick skillet with nonstick coating. Preheat over medium-high heat. Add half of the meat mixture. Cook and stir for 2 to 3 minutes or to desired doneness. Remove meat from skillet. Repeat with remaining meat mixture (add 1 teaspoon cooking oil if necessary). Remove meat from skillet, reserving juices in skillet.

Add the pepper strips and onion wedges to juices in skillet. Bring to boiling; reduce heat. Cover and simmer for 3 to 4 minutes or till vegetables are crisp-tender. Stir the meat into vegetables. Heat through.

To serve, place about ½ cup of the meat mixture on each tortilla. Roll up. Makes 5 servings.

Nutrition information per serving: 388 calories, 24 g protein, 45 g carbohydrate, 12 g fat (4 g saturated), 43 mg cholesterol, 541 mg sodium.

Midwest Swiss Steak with Tomato Gravy

Serve this satisfying entrée with a tossed green salad and crusty sourdough rolls.

1½	pounds boneless beef round steak
2	tablespoons all-purpose flour
	Nonstick spray coating
2	large onions, sliced
2	cups chopped peeled parsnips
1	14½-ounce can low-sodium tomatoes, cut up
1	large red sweet pepper, chopped
1	cup beef broth
1	teaspoon salt-free seasoning blend
1	teaspoon dried basil, crushed
1	clove garlic, minced
¼	teaspoon black pepper
1	tablespoon cold water
1	teaspoon cornstarch
2	tablespoons snipped parsley

Trim fat from meat. Cut meat into 6 serving-size pieces. Sprinkle both sides of meat with flour. With a meat mallet, pound the flour into meat.

Spray an unheated 12-inch skillet with nonstick coating. Preheat over medium heat. Add meat and cook till brown on both sides. Add the onions, parsnips, undrained tomatoes, sweet pepper, beef broth, seasoning blend, basil, garlic, and black pepper. Bring to boiling; reduce heat. Cover and simmer about 1¼ hours or till meat and vegetables are tender. Transfer meat and vegetables to a platter. Cover and keep warm while preparing sauce.

For sauce, skim fat from pan drippings. Stir together water and cornstarch. Stir into pan drippings. Cook and stir till thickened and bubbly. Cook and stir for 2 minutes more. Stir in parsley. Serve sauce over meat and vegetables. Makes 6 servings.

Nutrition information per serving: 211 calories, 25 g protein, 16 g carbohydrate, 5 g fat (2 g saturated), 60 mg cholesterol, 321 mg sodium.

Peppered Steak with Mushroom Gravy

Tenderloin is one of the leanest cuts of beef. To keep these prized steaks at their moist and juicy best, don't overcook them.

6	beef tenderloin steaks or 3 beef top loin steaks, cut 1 inch thick (about 1½ pounds total)
1½	teaspoons dried whole green peppercorns, crushed, or ½ teaspoon coarsely ground black pepper
½	teaspoon dried thyme, crushed
½	teaspoon dried oregano, crushed
¼	teaspoon salt
	Nonstick spray coating
⅓	cup water
½	teaspoon instant beef bouillon granules
¾	cup sliced fresh shiitake mushrooms or other fresh mushrooms
¾	cup fat-free milk
2	tablespoons all-purpose flour
½	teaspoon dried thyme, crushed
⅔	cup fat-free or light dairy sour cream
	Fresh thyme sprigs (optional)

Trim fat from steaks. In a small bowl stir together the peppercorns or pepper, ½ teaspoon dried thyme, oregano, and salt. Sprinkle both sides of steaks with pepper mixture, pressing into meat.

Spray an unheated large nonstick skillet with nonstick coating. Preheat over medium heat. Add steaks and cook to desired doneness, turning once. (Allow 8 to 11 minutes for medium rare or 12 to 14 minutes for medium.) Remove from skillet. Cover and keep warm.

For sauce, add water and bouillon granules to skillet. Bring to boiling. Add the mushrooms. Cook about 2 minutes or till tender. Stir together milk, flour, and ½ teaspoon dried thyme. Add to mushroom mixture. Cook and stir till thickened and bubbly. Stir in sour cream. Heat through, but do not boil.

To serve, spoon the sauce over steaks. If desired, garnish with fresh thyme. Makes 6 servings.

Nutrition information per serving: 206 calories, 25 g protein, 9 g carbohydrate, 7 g fat (3 g saturated), 64 mg cholesterol, 243 mg sodium.

Spaghetti with Italian Meatballs

We trimmed the fat in this dish simply by using lean ground beef and adding not a speck of fat to the sauce.
Our slimmed-down version saves 10 grams of fat per serving compared to the more traditional dish.

½	cup soft bread crumbs
1	slightly beaten egg white
2	tablespoons finely chopped onion
1½	teaspoons dried Italian seasoning, crushed
¼	teaspoon fennel seed, crushed
⅛	teaspoon salt
⅛	teaspoon ground red pepper
8	ounces extra-lean ground beef
8	ounces packaged dried spaghetti
	Nonstick spray coating
2	cups sliced fresh mushrooms
⅔	cup chopped onion
4	cloves garlic, minced
1	28-ounce can crushed tomatoes
½	cup water
½	of a 6-ounce can (⅓ cup) low-sodium tomato paste
½	teaspoon sugar
¼	teaspoon black pepper
	Finely shredded Parmesan cheese (optional)

For meatballs, in a medium mixing bowl stir together the bread crumbs, egg white, the 2 tablespoons onion, ¼ teaspoon of the Italian seasoning, fennel seed, salt, and ground red pepper. Add ground beef; mix well. Shape into 16 meatballs. Place meatballs in a 2-quart square baking dish. Bake, uncovered, in a 375° oven about 20 minutes or till no longer pink. Drain fat.

Meanwhile, cook the pasta according to package directions. Drain; keep warm.

For sauce, spray an unheated large saucepan with nonstick coating. Preheat over medium heat. Add mushrooms, the ⅔ cup onion, and garlic and cook for 3 to 4 minutes or till tender. Stir in crushed tomatoes, water, tomato paste, sugar, black pepper, and the remaining Italian seasoning.

Bring to boiling; reduce heat. Cover and simmer for 15 minutes. Gently stir cooked meatballs into sauce. Heat through. To serve, spoon meatball mixture over hot pasta. If desired, sprinkle with Parmesan cheese. Makes 4 servings.

Nutrition information per serving: 431 calories, 24 g protein, 66 g carbohydrate, 8 g fat (3 g saturated), 41 mg cholesterol, 474 mg sodium.

Bolognese Meat Sauce with Pasta

Traditionally, Bolognese (boh-luh-NEEZ) sauce is full of meat. We've cut back on fat and calories by substituting lentils for part of the meat.

2 tablespoons finely chopped pancetta (Italian bacon) (optional)

12 ounces extra-lean ground beef

2 14½-ounce cans low-sodium tomatoes, cut up

1 cup chopped onion

¾ cup dry lentils

¼ cup finely chopped carrot

¼ cup finely chopped celery

¼ cup snipped Italian flat-leaf or regular parsley

¼ cup tomato paste

1 teaspoon instant beef bouillon granules

1 cup water

½ cup dry white wine or beef broth

12 ounces packaged dried pasta (such as mostaccioli or spaghetti)

⅓ cup evaporated fat-free milk

Grated Parmesan cheese (optional)

Italian flat-leaf parsley sprigs (optional)

In a large saucepan or Dutch oven cook pancetta (if using) just till crisp. Add ground beef. Cook till meat is no longer pink. Drain fat.

If desired, pass undrained tomatoes through a food mill or sieve. (Or, process in blender or food processor till nearly smooth.) For sauce, add the tomatoes, onion, lentils, carrot, celery, snipped parsley, tomato paste, and bouillon granules to meat in saucepan. Stir in the water and wine or broth.

Bring to boiling; reduce heat. Cover and simmer about 40 minutes or till the lentils are tender, stirring occasionally. Uncover and simmer about 5 minutes more or till of desired consistency.

Meanwhile, cook the pasta according to package directions. Drain; keep warm.

Stir evaporated milk into meat mixture. Heat through. Serve the sauce over hot pasta. If desired, sprinkle with Parmesan cheese and garnish with parsley sprigs. Makes 6 servings.

Nutrition information per serving: 447 calories, 27 g protein, 64 g carbohydrate, 8 g fat (3 g saturated), 41 mg cholesterol, 314 mg sodium.

Grilled Apricot-Stuffed Pork Chops

The tangy flavor of apricots pairs deliciously with the smoky taste of grilled pork.

4   pork center loin chops, cut 1 inch
        thick
½   cup cooked brown rice or long grain
        rice
¼   cup snipped dried apricots
¼   cup finely chopped onion
1   tablespoon reduced-calorie apricot
        spread
¼   teaspoon dried thyme, crushed
¼   teaspoon pepper
¼   cup reduced-calorie apricot spread

Trim fat from chops. Make a pocket in each chop by cutting horizontally from the fat side almost to the bone. For stuffing, in a medium mixing bowl stir together the rice, apricots, onion, the 1 tablespoon apricot spread, thyme, and pepper. Spoon stuffing into each pocket. If necessary, secure the openings with wooden toothpicks.

In a covered grill arrange medium-hot coals around a drip pan. Test for medium heat above the pan. Place chops on grill rack over drip pan. Cover and grill for 30 to 40 minutes or till chops are slightly pink in center and juices run clear, turning once.

(Or, place chops on the greased unheated rack of a broiler pan. Broil 4 inches from the heat for 22 to 27 minutes, turning once.)

Meanwhile, in a small saucepan heat the ¼ cup apricot spread till melted. Brush over chops the last 5 minutes of cooking. Makes 4 servings.

Nutrition information per serving: 208 calories, 16 g protein, 19 g carbohydrate, 7 g fat (2 g saturated), 48 mg cholesterol, 59 mg sodium.

Italian Pot Roast

Fresh pork is light pink in color. When this roast reaches the desired 155° internal temperature, the meat will be slightly pink, but when a small cut is made in the meat, the juices should run clear.

1 1½- to 2-pound boneless pork top loin roast (single loin)
2 teaspoons snipped fresh rosemary or 1 teaspoon dried rosemary, crushed
1 teaspoon olive oil or cooking oil
1 clove garlic, minced
1 cup apple juice
⅓ cup sliced leek or chopped onion
1 small Golden Delicious or Granny Smith apple, cored and chopped
2 teaspoons cornstarch
2 tablespoons white wine vinegar
¼ teaspoon salt
⅛ teaspoon pepper

Trim fat from meat. In a small bowl combine the rosemary, olive or cooking oil, and garlic. Rub evenly over meat. Place the meat on a rack in a shallow roasting pan. Insert a meat thermometer into the center of meat.

Roast, uncovered, in a 325° oven for 1 to 1½ hours or till the meat thermometer registers 155°. Transfer the meat to a warm platter and cover with foil. Let stand while preparing the sauce. (The meat's temperature will rise 5° during standing.)

For sauce, reserve 2 tablespoons of the pan drippings. In a medium saucepan bring ¾ cup of the apple juice to boiling. Add leek or onion and apple; reduce heat. Cover and simmer about 4 minutes or just till tender.

Stir together the remaining apple juice and cornstarch. Stir into leek mixture. Stir in reserved pan drippings, vinegar, salt, and pepper. Cook and stir till thickened and bubbly. Cook and stir for 2 minutes more.

To serve, cut meat into slices and pass sauce with meat. Makes 6 to 8 servings.

Nutrition information per serving: 222 calories, 25 g protein, 9 g carbohydrate, 9 g fat (3 g saturated), 69 mg cholesterol, 142 mg sodium.

Mustard-Orange Pork Tenderloin

A mixture of vegetables, such as cut-up red onions, baby carrots, and chunks of zucchini, can be roasted alongside the meat. Just spray the vegetables with olive oil-flavored nonstick spray coating before placing them in the pan around the meat.

12 ounces pork tenderloin
½ cup apricot preserves or orange
    marmalade
3 tablespoons Dijon-style mustard
    Nonstick spray coating
2 cups sliced fresh mushrooms
½ cup sliced green onions
2 tablespoons orange juice

Trim fat from meat. Place meat on a rack in a shallow roasting pan. Insert a meat thermometer into the center of meat. Roast, uncovered, in a 425° oven for 10 minutes.

Meanwhile, in a small bowl stir together preserves or marmalade and mustard. Spoon half of the mustard mixture over the meat. Set the remaining mustard mixture aside.

Roast for 15 to 25 minutes more or till the meat thermometer registers 155°. Transfer the meat to a warm platter and cover with foil. Let stand for 10 minutes before slicing. (The meat's temperature will rise 5° during standing.)

Meanwhile, spray a medium saucepan with nonstick coating. Add mushrooms and green onions. Cook and stir for 2 to 3 minutes or till mushrooms are tender. Stir in the remaining mustard mixture and orange juice. Cook and stir till heated through.

To serve, thinly slice the meat. Spoon the mushroom mixture over meat. Makes 4 servings.

Nutrition information per serving: 240 calories, 21 g protein, 32 g carbohydrate, 4 g fat (1 g saturated), 60 mg cholesterol, 334 mg sodium.

Peppered Pork & Apricot Salad

Dazzle guests with a main-dish salad whose vibrant colors—bright green, apricot, and black and cream— make a statement on the serving plates. Use quick-cooking pork tenderloin, then slice it into appealing medallions. (Also pictured on the cover.)

12 ounces pork tenderloin
1 teaspoon coarsely ground pepper
1 6-ounce package long-grain and
   wild rice mix
½ cup snipped dried apricots
¼ cup fat-free Italian salad dressing
2 green onions, thinly sliced
2 tablespoons frozen orange juice
   concentrate, thawed
½ cup frozen peas
   Fresh apricots, pitted and sliced
   (optional)

Trim fat from meat. Place meat on a rack in a shallow roasting pan. Sprinkle the meat with pepper. Insert a meat thermometer into the center of meat. Roast, uncovered, in a 425° oven for 25 to 35 minutes or till the meat thermometer registers 155°. Remove from oven and cover with foil. Let stand for 10 minutes.

Meanwhile, prepare rice mix according to package directions, adding the dried apricots during the last 5 minutes of cooking. Spread mixture in a shallow baking pan and cool for 20 minutes.

For dressing, in a small bowl combine salad dressing, green onions, and orange juice concentrate. In a large bowl combine rice mixture and peas. Drizzle with dressing. Toss gently to coat. Spoon rice mixture onto dinner plates. Cut meat crosswise into thin slices; arrange meat on rice mixture. If desired, garnish with fresh apricots. Makes 4 servings.

Nutrition information per serving: 356 calories, 25 g protein, 50 g carbohydrate, 6 g fat (2 g saturated), 61 mg cholesterol, 1,056 mg sodium.

Snipping Apricots Made Easy

To snip dried apricots quickly and easily, place apricot halves in a 1-cup glass measure and use kitchen shears or scissors to snip the fruit. Dipping the shears in cold water between snips will keep the apricot pieces from sticking to the shears.

Spicy Pork Chops

Vegetable juice is the base for this zippy marinade. Try the hot-style version, which will give you extra heat.

4   boneless pork loin chops, cut
      ½ inch thick (about 1¼ pounds
      total)
1   6-ounce can (¾ cup) vegetable juice
2   tablespoons sliced green onion
2   tablespoons canned diced green
      chili peppers
1   teaspoon Worcestershire sauce
1   clove garlic, minced
½   teaspoon dried basil, crushed
      Few dashes bottled hot pepper sauce
2   cups hot cooked orzo or rice

Trim fat from chops. Place chops in a plastic bag and set the bag into a shallow bowl.

For marinade, in a small bowl combine the vegetable juice, green onion, chili peppers, Worcestershire sauce, garlic, basil, and hot pepper sauce. Pour over chops; seal bag. Marinate in the refrigerator for 2 to 24 hours, turning bag occasionally.

Drain chops, reserving marinade. Place chops on the unheated rack of a broiler pan. Broil 3 to 4 inches from the heat for 5 to 7 minutes or till chops are slightly pink in center and juices run clear, turning once. In a small saucepan bring the marinade to boiling. Boil gently, uncovered, for 1 minute.

Serve the hot marinade with the pork chops and hot orzo or rice. Makes 4 servings.

Nutrition information per serving: 273 calories, 22 g protein, 21 g carbohydrate, 11 g fat (4 g saturated), 63 mg cholesterol, 241 mg sodium.

Broiling Basics

To make sure food is placed correctly for even broiling, use a ruler to measure the distance from the surface of the food to the heating element. If the distance does not match the guidelines in your recipe, adjust the broiler pan or oven rack. *Be sure to measure before turning on the broiler.* To keep clean up to a minimum, line the broiler pan with foil before sliding the broiler rack into position.

Lamb Chops and Peppers

Enjoy this quick-cooking skillet dish in the summertime, when sweet peppers and zucchini are at their peak.

4 lamb leg sirloin chops, cut ¾ inch thick (about 1¼ pounds total)
Nonstick spray coating
1 medium green sweet pepper, cut into julienne strips
1 medium red or yellow sweet pepper, cut into julienne strips
1 small zucchini, cut into julienne strips
½ cup thinly sliced leek
1 clove garlic, minced
½ cup dry white wine or water
1 teaspoon instant beef bouillon granules
1 teaspoon dried basil, crushed
½ teaspoon dried oregano, crushed
⅛ teaspoon black pepper

Trim fat from chops. Spray an unheated large nonstick skillet with nonstick coating. Preheat over medium-high heat. Add the chops and cook about 4 minutes or till browned, turning once. Remove chops from skillet, reserving drippings in skillet.

Add the sweet peppers, zucchini, leek, and garlic to reserved drippings. Cook and stir for 3 minutes. Return the chops to skillet.

In a small mixing bowl stir together wine or water, bouillon granules, basil, oregano, and black pepper. Pour over zucchini mixture.

Bring to boiling; reduce heat. Cover and simmer for 8 to 10 minutes or till chops are slightly pink in center. Makes 4 servings.

Nutrition information per serving: 181 calories, 19 g protein, 8 g carbohydrate, 6 g fat (2 g saturated), 58 mg cholesterol, 268 mg sodium.

Apricot-Stuffed Grilled Turkey Breast

Here's a tip from our Test Kitchen: Use kitchen scissors to snip the dried apricots. It's easier, faster, and less messy than a knife and cutting board.

1	2- to 2½-pound bone-in turkey breast half
1½	cups soft bread crumbs (2 slices)
½	cup snipped dried apricots
¼	cup chopped pecans, toasted
2	tablespoons apple juice or water
1	tablespoon cooking oil
¼	teaspoon dried rosemary, crushed
¼	teaspoon garlic salt
1	tablespoon Dijon-style mustard
1	tablespoon water

Remove bone from turkey breast. Rinse turkey; pat dry with paper towels. Cut a horizontal slit into the thickest part of turkey breast to form a 5x4-inch pocket. Set aside.

For stuffing, in a medium mixing bowl combine bread crumbs, apricots, pecans, apple juice or water, oil, rosemary, and garlic salt. Spoon stuffing into pocket. Securely fasten the opening with wooden toothpicks or tie with 100% cotton string. Stir together mustard and water; set aside.

In a covered grill arrange medium-hot coals around a drip pan. Test for medium heat above the pan. Place turkey on grill rack over drip pan. Cover and grill about 1 hour or till turkey juices run clear (stuffing should reach 160°). Brush with the mustard mixture during the last 15 minutes of grilling.

Remove turkey from grill and cover with foil. Let stand for 15 minutes before slicing. Makes 8 servings.

Nutrition information per serving: 237 calories, 24 g protein, 10 g carbohydrate, 11 g fat (2 g saturated), 59 mg cholesterol, 205 mg sodium.

Roasted Peppers and Chicken Skillet

Roasted peppers add color and sweetness to this dish, but they're also an outstanding source of vitamin A. Make them up ahead (see note, below) to save time when preparing this dish.

2   large yellow, red, and/or green
    sweet peppers
2   pounds meaty chicken pieces
    (breasts, thighs, and drumsticks)
1   tablespoon olive oil
1   teaspoon dried oregano, crushed
¼   teaspoon salt
    Dash crushed red pepper
1   cup chopped onion
¾   cup thinly sliced celery
¾   cup dry white wine or reduced-
    sodium chicken broth
1   14½-ounce can tomatoes, cut up
2   cups hot cooked rice

To roast the sweet peppers, cut them into quarters. Remove stems, seeds, and membranes. Place pepper pieces, cut sides down, on a baking sheet lined with foil. Roast in a 425° oven for 20 to 25 minutes or till skins are bubbly and very dark. Wrap pepper pieces tightly in foil and let stand for 10 to 15 minutes or till cool enough to handle. Using a paring knife, pull the skin off gently. Cut into ½-inch-wide strips. Set aside.

Skin chicken. Rinse chicken; pat dry with paper towels. In a large nonstick skillet cook chicken in hot oil over medium heat for 10 to 15 minutes or till lightly browned, turning to brown evenly. Drain fat. Sprinkle with oregano, salt, and crushed red pepper. Stir in the onion, celery, and wine or chicken broth. Bring to boiling.

Cook, uncovered, over high heat for 10 to 15 minutes or till most of the liquid has evaporated, turning chicken once. Carefully stir in undrained tomatoes.

Cover and simmer for 15 minutes. Stir in the roasted pepper strips. Cook, uncovered, about 5 minutes more or till chicken is tender and no longer pink and sauce is of desired consistency. Serve over hot cooked rice. Makes 4 servings.

Note: To prepare the roasted sweet peppers ahead, roast as directed and place the pepper strips and a small amount of olive oil in an airtight container. Refrigerate for up to 1 week.

Nutrition information per serving: 441 calories, 36 g protein, 43 g carbohydrate, 10 g fat (2 g saturated), 93 mg cholesterol, 411 mg sodium.

Grilled Chicken and Vegetable Kabobs

If you place the vegetables and chicken on separate skewers, you won't have to worry about the vegetables becoming overcooked before the chicken is done—just remove each skewer when it is perfectly cooked.

1 pound skinless, boneless chicken
  breast halves
4 medium fresh mushrooms
3 green onions, cut into 1-inch pieces
1 medium red, orange, yellow, and/or
  green sweet pepper, cut into
  1½-inch pieces
¼ cup salsa
¼ cup catsup
2 tablespoons jalapeño jelly
  Hot cooked rice (optional)
  Thinly sliced green onion (optional)
  Fresh rosemary sprigs (optional)

Rinse chicken; pat dry with paper towels. Cut chicken lengthwise into ½-inch-wide strips. On 2 long or 4 short skewers, loosely thread chicken accordion-style. On 1 long or 2 short skewers, alternately thread the mushrooms and green onion pieces, and on 1 long or 2 short skewers, thread the sweet pepper pieces.

For sauce, in a small saucepan combine salsa, catsup, and jelly. Cook and stir till heated through and jelly is melted. Brush over chicken and vegetables.

Grill skewers on an uncovered grill directly over medium coals for 10 to 12 minutes or till chicken is tender and no longer pink and vegetables are crisp-tender, turning and brushing once with sauce.

(Or, place skewers on the unheated rack of a broiler pan. Broil 4 to 5 inches from the heat for 10 to 12 minutes, turning once and brushing with sauce.)

If desired, toss hot rice with thinly sliced green onion. Serve skewers on rice mixture and, if desired, garnish with rosemary. Makes 4 servings.

Nutrition information per serving: 183 calories, 23 g protein, 15 g carbohydrate, 4 g fat (1 g saturated), 59 mg cholesterol, 314 mg sodium.

Jamaican Jerk Chicken

If you like, you can use 1 tablespoon purchased Jamaican Jerk seasoning in place of the crushed red pepper, salt, allspice, curry powder, black pepper, thyme, and ginger.

4 medium skinless, boneless
    chicken breast halves
    (about 1 pound total)
½ cup coarsely chopped onion
2 tablespoons lime juice
2 cloves garlic, quartered
1 teaspoon crushed red pepper
½ teaspoon salt
½ teaspoon ground allspice
¼ teaspoon curry powder
¼ teaspoon coarsely ground black
    pepper
⅛ teaspoon dried thyme, crushed
⅛ teaspoon ground ginger
1 medium red, yellow, or green sweet
    pepper, cut into 1½-inch pieces
1 small zucchini, sliced ½ inch thick
1 tablespoon cooking oil
¼ teaspoon coarsely ground
    black pepper

Rinse chicken; pat dry with paper towels. Place chicken in a shallow dish.

In a blender container combine the onion, lime juice, garlic, crushed red pepper, salt, allspice, curry powder, ¼ teaspoon black pepper, thyme, and ginger. Cover and blend till smooth. Spoon over chicken, turning to coat both sides. Cover and chill for 30 minutes.

Meanwhile, on four 8- to 10-inch skewers, alternately thread sweet pepper and zucchini pieces. Brush with oil and sprinkle with ¼ teaspoon black pepper.

Drain chicken, reserving spice mixture. Grill chicken on an uncovered grill directly over medium coals for 12 to 15 minutes or till tender and no longer pink, turning and brushing once with spice mixture. Add vegetables to the grill during the last 10 minutes of grilling, turning frequently. Makes 4 servings.

Nutrition information per serving: 176 calories, 22 g protein, 6 g carbohydrate, 7 g fat (1 g saturated), 59 mg cholesterol, 327 mg sodium.

Test the Temperature

Before you grill, check the temperature of the coals. Hold your hand, palm side down, in the location you plan to place the food. Count "one thousand one, one thousand two," etc., for as long as you can hold your hand there. Two seconds means the coals are hot, three is medium-hot, four is medium, five is medium-slow, and six is slow.

Easy Orange-Glazed Chicken

Serve this flavorful chicken with wild rice and steamed fresh asparagus for a healthful meal.

4   medium skinless, boneless chicken
      breast halves (about 1 pound
      total)
      Several dashes paprika
      Nonstick spray coating
½   of a 6-ounce can (⅓ cup) frozen
      orange juice concentrate, thawed
2   teaspoons snipped fresh rosemary or
      thyme or ½ teaspoon dried
      rosemary or thyme, crushed

Rinse chicken; pat dry with paper towels. Sprinkle with paprika. Spray an unheated large nonstick skillet with nonstick coating. Preheat over medium heat.

Add chicken and cook about 4 minutes or till brown, turning once. Meanwhile, for glaze, stir together the orange juice concentrate and herb. Spoon over chicken. Cover and cook for 5 to 6 minutes more or till chicken is tender and no longer pink. To serve, spoon glaze over chicken. Makes 4 servings.

Nutrition information per serving: 166 calories, 22 g protein, 11 g carbohydrate, 4 g fat (1 g saturated), 59 mg cholesterol, 55 mg sodium.

Fruity Chicken Salad Sandwiches

For a special touch, pick up a specialty wheat bread from your favorite bakery.

2   cups chopped cooked chicken breast
      (10 ounces)
1   small Red Delicious or Granny
      Smith apple, cored and chopped
⅓   cup sliced celery
¼   cup raisins
1   green onion, thinly sliced
¼   cup plain fat-free yogurt
¼   cup reduced-calorie ranch salad
      dressing
      Red-tipped leaf lettuce
8   slices whole wheat or other bread

In a large mixing bowl stir together the chicken, apple, celery, raisins, and green onion. In a small bowl combine yogurt and ranch salad dressing. Pour over chicken mixture; toss gently to coat.

Arrange lettuce leaves on half of the bread slices. Spread chicken mixture on lettuce. Top with the remaining bread. Makes 4 servings.

Nutrition information per serving: 332 calories, 29 g protein, 38 g carbohydrate, 8 g fat (1 g saturated), 65 mg cholesterol, 590 mg sodium.

Fruity Chicken Salad Sandwiches

Hot 'n' Sweet Barbecued Chicken

Stir together just six ingredients for this finger-licking sauce—no simmering needed.

¼ cup salsa
¼ cup catsup
¼ cup orange marmalade
 1 tablespoon vinegar
½ teaspoon chili powder
½ teaspoon Worcestershire sauce
 2 to 2½ pounds meaty chicken pieces
    (breasts, thighs, and drumsticks)

For sauce, in a small mixing bowl stir together salsa, catsup, orange marmalade, vinegar, chili powder, and Worcestershire sauce. Set aside.

Skin chicken. Rinse chicken; pat dry with paper towels. In a covered grill arrange medium-hot coals around a drip pan. Test for medium heat above the pan. Place chicken on grill rack over drip pan. Cover and grill for 50 to 60 minutes or till chicken is tender and no longer pink. Brush chicken generously with sauce during the last 10 minutes of grilling.

(Or, arrange chicken in a 2-quart rectangular baking dish. Bake, uncovered, in a 375° oven for 30 minutes. Brush generously with the sauce. Bake for 10 to 15 minutes more or till tender and no longer pink.)

Transfer chicken to a warm platter. Makes 4 servings.

Nutrition information per serving: 267 calories, 30 g protein, 20 g carbohydrate, 8 g fat (2 g saturated), 92 mg cholesterol, 353 mg sodium.

Turkey Taco Salad

Canned beans that have no salt added will save about 160 mg sodium per serving.

Nonstick spray coating
12 ounces lean ground raw turkey
    or chicken
1 15½-ounce can dark red kidney
    beans, rinsed and drained
1 14½-ounce can low-sodium
    tomatoes, cut up
1 4-ounce can diced green chili
    peppers, drained
1 tablespoon chili powder
½ teaspoon ground cumin
4 cups torn mixed greens
½ cup shredded reduced-fat cheddar
    cheese (2 ounces)
¼ cup fat-free dairy sour cream or
    plain fat-free yogurt
    Baked tortilla chips (optional)

Spray an unheated large skillet with nonstick coating. Preheat over medium heat. Add the turkey or chicken and cook about 5 minutes or till no longer pink. Drain fat, if necessary.

Stir the red kidney beans, undrained tomatoes, green chili peppers, chili powder, and cumin into cooked turkey. Bring to boiling; reduce heat. Cover and simmer for 3 minutes.

Uncover skillet. Return to boiling; reduce heat. Simmer, uncovered, for 5 to 10 minutes more or till of desired consistency.

Meanwhile, arrange mixed greens on dinner plates. Spoon the hot turkey mixture over greens. Sprinkle with cheese and top with sour cream or yogurt. If desired, serve with tortilla chips. Makes 4 servings.

Nutrition information per serving: 291 calories, 26 g protein, 28 g carbohydrate, 11 g fat (3 g saturated), 42 mg cholesterol, 439 mg sodium.

Shopping for Ground Turkey

Cooking with the leanest ground turkey available can help cut down the fat content of dishes such as Turkey Taco Salad (above). At the supermarket, read the package labels carefully. Select ground turkey that's at least 90 percent lean by weight. If the fat content isn't listed on the label, look at the turkey itself. If it has lots of white specks, it probably means that fat and skin have been ground up with the meat. For the leanest ground turkey, purchase ground turkey breast or ask your butcher to grind a turkey breast for you.

Chicken and Biscuit Pie

Nonfat dry milk powder makes a creamy gravy in this hearty one-dish meal.

1½ pounds whole chicken breasts,
      halved lengthwise
2¼ cups water
  1 bay leaf
  2 cups cubed peeled potatoes
      (2 medium)
  1 cup chopped onion
  ½ cup nonfat dry milk powder
  5 tablespoons all-purpose flour
  1 teaspoon dried basil, crushed
  ¾ teaspoon poultry seasoning
  ¼ teaspoon salt
  ⅛ teaspoon pepper
  1 cup frozen peas
      Green Onion Biscuits

Skin chicken. Rinse chicken; pat dry with paper towels. In a 4-quart Dutch oven combine chicken, water, and bay leaf. Bring to boiling; reduce heat. Cover and simmer for 20 to 25 minutes or till chicken is tender and no longer pink. Drain, reserving cooking liquid. Discard bay leaf. Cool chicken slightly. Cut chicken into bite-size pieces; discard bones.

Meanwhile, in a large saucepan cook potatoes and onion in a small amount of boiling water about 10 minutes or till potatoes are tender. Drain; return to saucepan. Keep warm.

For sauce, in a small saucepan stir together the dry milk powder, flour, basil, poultry seasoning, salt, and pepper. Add 2 cups of the reserved cooking liquid, stirring till smooth. Cook and stir over medium heat till thickened and bubbly. Gently stir the sauce, cooked chicken, and peas into the potato mixture. Keep warm while preparing the Green Onion Biscuits.

Spoon chicken mixture into four 14-ounce individual casseroles or a 2-quart rectangular baking dish. Drop biscuit dough into 8 mounds onto warm mixture. Bake in a 400° oven for 20 to 25 minutes or till biscuits are golden and a wooden toothpick inserted into biscuits comes out clean. Makes 4 servings.

Green Onion Biscuits: Stir together ⅔ cup *all-purpose flour;* 1 tablespoon thinly sliced *green onion;* 1 teaspoon *baking powder;* 1 teaspoon *sugar;* ¼ teaspoon dried *basil,* crushed; and dash *salt.* Stir together ⅓ cup *fat-free milk* and 4 teaspoons *cooking oil.* Stir into flour mixture just till combined.

Nutrition information per serving: 462 calories, 32 g protein, 52 g carbohydrate, 14 g fat (3 g saturated), 61 mg cholesterol, 315 mg sodium.

Grilled Tuna with Tuscan Beans

Tuna and beans—tonno e fagioli—is a favorite combination in Italian coastal towns. Using canned beans makes our version fast and easy.

1   pound fresh or frozen tuna, swordfish, halibut, shark, or salmon steaks

2   cloves garlic, minced

1   tablespoon olive oil

1   14½-ounce can Italian-style stewed tomatoes, cut up

2   teaspoons snipped fresh sage or ¼ teaspoon ground sage

1   15-ounce can small white beans, rinsed and drained

2   teaspoons olive oil

2   teaspoons lemon juice

⅛   teaspoon pepper

    Fresh sage sprigs (optional)

Thaw fish, if frozen. In a large skillet cook the garlic in 1 tablespoon hot oil for 15 seconds. Stir in the undrained tomatoes and snipped fresh or dried sage. Bring to boiling; reduce heat. Simmer, uncovered, for 5 minutes. Stir in beans; heat through.

Meanwhile, rinse fish; pat dry with paper towels. Cut fish into 4 serving-size portions. Brush both sides of fish with the 2 teaspoons oil and the lemon juice. Sprinkle with pepper.

Grill fish on the greased rack of an uncovered grill directly over medium coals till fish flakes easily with a fork, gently turning once (allow 4 to 6 minutes per ½-inch thickness).

[Or, place fish on the greased unheated rack of a broiler pan. Broil 4 inches from heat, gently turning once (allow 4 to 6 minutes per ½-inch thickness).]

To serve, remove the skin from fish. Spoon the bean mixture onto dinner plates and top with fish. If desired, garnish with sage sprigs. Makes 4 servings.

Nutrition information per serving: 298 calories, 33 g protein, 25 g carbohydrate, 7 g fat (1 g saturated), 49 mg cholesterol, 536 mg sodium.

Fish Fillets with Red Pepper Sauce

Use these tips when you choose fresh fish: Make sure the fish in the counter is displayed on a bed of ice. The fish should have a mild smell, not a strong fishy odor. Avoid fish that is dry around the edges.

3 medium red sweet peppers, chopped, or one 12-ounce jar roasted red sweet peppers, drained and chopped
2 cloves garlic, minced
2 teaspoons olive oil
½ cup water
⅓ cup loosely packed snipped fresh basil or 1 teaspoon dried basil, crushed
2 tablespoons tomato paste
1 tablespoon red wine vinegar
½ teaspoon sugar
⅛ teaspoon salt
   Dash black pepper
1 pound fresh or frozen fish fillets
¼ cup water
1 lemon, sliced

For sauce, in a large skillet cook fresh sweet peppers and garlic in hot oil over medium heat for 20 minutes, stirring occasionally. (Or, if using peppers from a jar, in a medium saucepan cook garlic in hot oil for 30 to 60 seconds or till light brown. Stir in peppers; remove from heat.)

Place the pepper mixture in a blender container or food processor bowl. Cover and blend or process till nearly smooth. Add the ½ cup water, basil, tomato paste, vinegar, sugar, salt, and black pepper. Cover and blend or process with several on-off turns just till nearly smooth. Return to the skillet. Cook and stir over medium heat till heated through.

Meanwhile, rinse fresh or frozen fish; pat dry with paper towels. In another large skillet bring the ¼ cup water and half of the lemon slices just to boiling. Carefully add fish. Return just to boiling; reduce heat. Cover and simmer till fish flakes easily with a fork (allow 4 to 6 minutes per ½-inch thickness for fresh fish; 6 to 9 minutes per ½-inch thickness for frozen fish). Remove fish from skillet.

To serve, spoon some of the sauce onto dinner plates. Place the fish on top of sauce. Garnish with the remaining lemon slices. Freeze any remaining sauce for another time. Makes 4 servings.

Nutrition information per serving: 154 calories, 23 g protein, 8 g carbohydrate, 3 g fat (1 g saturated), 54 mg cholesterol, 195 mg sodium.

Salmon with Wilted Greens

This fish dinner packs in all the vitamin C and almost half of the vitamin A you need for an entire day—all for under 300 calories.

4 fresh or frozen salmon steaks, cut ¾ inch thick (about 1 pound)
3 tablespoons orange juice concentrate
3 tablespoons water
2 tablespoons reduced-sodium soy sauce
1 tablespoon honey
2 teaspoons cooking oil
1 teaspoon toasted sesame oil
½ teaspoon grated gingerroot or ¼ teaspoon ground ginger
6 cups torn mixed greens (such as spinach, Swiss chard, radicchio, or mustard, beet, or collard greens)
1 small red sweet pepper, cut into thin strips
1 medium orange, peeled and sectioned
Orange peel strips (optional)

Thaw fish, if frozen. For dressing, in a small bowl combine orange juice concentrate, water, soy sauce, honey, cooking oil, sesame oil, and ginger.

Rinse fish; pat dry with paper towels. Place the fish on the greased unheated rack of a broiler pan. Broil 4 inches from the heat for 5 minutes. Using a wide spatula, carefully turn fish. Brush with 1 tablespoon of the dressing. Broil for 3 to 7 minutes more or till fish flakes easily with a fork.

(Or, grill fish on the greased rack of an uncovered grill directly over medium coals for 3 minutes. Carefully turn fish. Brush with 1 tablespoon of the dressing. Grill for 3 to 6 minutes more.)

Remove fish. Cover and keep warm. Place the greens in a large salad bowl. In a large skillet bring the remaining dressing to boiling. Add red pepper strips. Remove from heat. Pour over greens, tossing to coat.

To serve, divide greens mixture among dinner plates. Arrange the orange sections and fish on top of greens. If desired, garnish with orange peel strips. Serve immediately. Makes 4 servings.

Nutrition information per serving: 255 calories, 27 g protein, 15 g carbohydrate, 9 g fat (2 g saturated), 31 mg cholesterol, 406 mg sodium.

Sweet and Sour Mahimahi

You can make this marinade the night before and chill it in a covered jar.

4 fresh or frozen mahimahi, swordfish, or tuna steaks, cut ¾ inch thick (about 1 pound)
3 tablespoons rice wine or dry white wine
2 tablespoons dry sherry
1 tablespoon honey
2 teaspoons light soy sauce
1½ teaspoons grated gingerroot
2 cloves garlic, minced
⅛ teaspoon pepper
Hot cooked rice or egg noodles (optional)

Thaw fish, if frozen. Rinse fish; pat dry with paper towels. Place fish in a shallow nonmetal dish. For marinade, combine the wine, sherry, honey, soy sauce, gingerroot, garlic, and pepper. Pour over fish, turning to coat. Cover and marinate at room temperature for 30 minutes. Drain the fish, reserving marinade.

Place fish on the greased unheated rack of a broiler pan. Brush with some of the marinade. Broil 4 inches from the heat for 6 to 9 minutes or till fish flakes easily with a fork, gently turning once. Brush occasionally with marinade after 3 minutes of broiling. If desired, serve fish with hot rice or noodles. Makes 4 servings.

Nutrition information per serving: 134 calories, 21 g protein, 6 g carbohydrate, 1 g fat (0 g saturated), 83 mg cholesterol, 205 mg sodium.

Herbed Halibut

Try this fish served over steamed, julienned carrots and zucchini tossed with a bit of olive oil and Parmesan.

4 fresh or frozen halibut or salmon steaks, cut ¾ to 1 inch thick (1¼ to 1½ pounds)
⅓ cup chopped onion
1 clove garlic, minced
½ teaspoon dried basil, crushed
½ teaspoon dried chervil, crushed, or dried dillweed
⅛ teaspoon pepper
2 teaspoons cooking oil
¼ cup snipped parsley
⅓ cup plain fat-free yogurt

Thaw fish, if frozen. Rinse fish; pat dry with paper towels. In a small saucepan cook onion, garlic, basil, chervil or dillweed, and pepper in hot oil till onion is tender. Stir in parsley. Set aside.

Place fish on a greased rack in a shallow baking pan. Bake, uncovered, in a 400° oven for 10 minutes. Remove from oven. Spread fish with yogurt; sprinkle with herb mixture. Bake for 5 to 10 minutes more or till fish flakes easily with a fork. Makes 4 servings.

Nutrition information per serving: 195 calories, 31 g protein, 4 g carbohydrate, 6 g fat (1 g saturated), 46 mg cholesterol, 93 mg sodium.

Seafood Jambalaya

Cajun cooking comes to life here. Use purchased Cajun seasoning or mix up your own using the recipe below.

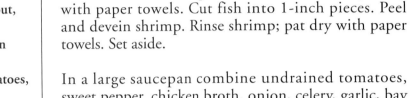

8 ounces fresh or frozen firm fish fillets or steaks (such as halibut, swordfish, or tuna)

8 ounces fresh or frozen shrimp in shells

1 28-ounce can low-sodium tomatoes, cut up

1½ cups chopped yellow, green, and/or red sweet pepper

1½ cups reduced-sodium chicken broth

1 cup chopped onion

1 cup sliced celery

2 cloves garlic, minced

1 bay leaf

1 teaspoon purchased or homemade Cajun seasoning

¼ teaspoon ground cloves

⅔ cup long grain rice

¼ cup snipped parsley

Celery leaves (optional)

Thaw fish and shrimp, if frozen. Rinse fish; pat dry with paper towels. Cut fish into 1-inch pieces. Peel and devein shrimp. Rinse shrimp; pat dry with paper towels. Set aside.

In a large saucepan combine undrained tomatoes, sweet pepper, chicken broth, onion, celery, garlic, bay leaf, Cajun seasoning, and cloves. Bring to boiling; reduce heat. Cover and simmer for 10 minutes.

Stir in the uncooked rice. Return to boiling; reduce heat. Cover and simmer for 15 minutes. Stir in fish and shrimp. Cook about 5 minutes more or till fish flakes easily with a fork and shrimp turn pink, stirring occasionally. Stir in the parsley. Discard bay leaf. If desired, garnish each serving with celery leaves. Makes 6 to 8 servings.

Homemade Cajun Seasoning: In a small mixing bowl combine 1 teaspoon *white pepper*, 1 teaspoon *garlic powder*, 1 teaspoon *onion powder*, 1 teaspoon *ground red pepper*, 1 teaspoon *paprika*, and 1 teaspoon *black pepper*. Store in an airtight container in a cool, dry place. Makes 2 tablespoons.

Nutrition information per serving: 200 calories, 17 g protein, 29 g carbohydrate, 2 g fat (0 g saturated), 56 mg cholesterol, 167 mg sodium.

Jalapeño Shrimp and Pasta

Rely on fresh jalapeños when you want to add spunk to a dish. To keep fresh peppers on hand for easy use, slice or chop them, then freeze them for up to 6 months.

12 ounces fresh or frozen shrimp
8 ounces packaged dried mostaccioli, rigatoni, or cavatelli
1 medium onion, chopped
1 jalapeño pepper, seeded and chopped
2 cloves garlic, minced
¼ teaspoon ground cumin
¼ teaspoon black pepper
⅛ teaspoon salt
1 tablespoon margarine or butter
2 medium tomatoes, chopped (1⅓ cups)
1 4-ounce can diced green chili peppers, drained
Jalapeño peppers (optional)

Thaw shrimp, if frozen. Cook the pasta according to package directions. Drain; keep warm. Meanwhile, peel and devein shrimp. Halve any large shrimp. Rinse shrimp; pat dry with paper towels.

In a large skillet cook shrimp, onion, chopped jalapeño pepper, garlic, cumin, black pepper, and salt in margarine or butter over medium-high heat for 1 to 3 minutes or till shrimp turn pink, stirring frequently.

Gently stir in the tomatoes and green chili peppers. Cook and stir over medium heat till heated through. Serve immediately over hot cooked pasta. If desired, garnish each serving with whole jalapeño peppers. Makes 4 servings.

Nutrition information per serving: 345 calories, 23 g protein, 51 g carbohydrate, 5 g fat (1 g saturated), 131 mg cholesterol, 338 mg sodium.

Selecting Shrimp

At fish markets or supermarket fish counters, shrimp is usually sold by the pound. The price per pound is determined by size—the bigger the shrimp, the higher the price and the fewer per pound. Select fresh shrimp that are moist and firm, have translucent flesh, and smell fresh. Signs of poor quality are an unpleasant ammonia odor and blackened edges or spots on the shells.

White Clam Sauce with Spaghetti

Italians generally do not top seafood sauces with grated cheese. For added texture, sprinkle on some toasted bread crumbs instead.

8 ounces packaged dried spaghetti,
    linguine, or fusilli
2 6½-ounce cans minced clams
½ cup chopped onion
2 cloves garlic, minced
2 teaspoons olive oil
¾ cup fat-free milk
⅓ cup all-purpose flour
¼ teaspoon salt
¼ teaspoon lemon-pepper seasoning
½ cup frozen peas
¼ cup snipped parsley
¼ cup dry white wine or chicken broth
1 tablespoon snipped fresh basil or
    ½ teaspoon dried basil, crushed
    Grated Parmesan cheese or bread
    crumbs, toasted (optional)

Cook pasta according to package directions. Drain; keep warm. Meanwhile, drain clams, reserving liquid. Set clams aside. Add enough water, if necessary, to the reserved liquid to make 1 cup. Set aside.

For sauce, in a medium saucepan cook the onion and garlic in hot oil till onion is tender. In a screw-top jar combine the milk and flour; shake till smooth.

Add the flour mixture, salt, lemon-pepper seasoning, and the reserved clam liquid to onion mixture. Cook and stir over medium heat till thickened and bubbly. Cook and stir for 1 minute more.

Stir in the clams, peas, parsley, wine or chicken broth, and basil. Heat through.

Serve the sauce over hot pasta. If desired, sprinkle each serving with Parmesan cheese or toasted bread crumbs. Makes 4 servings.

Nutrition information per serving: 404 calories, 24 g protein, 63 g carbohydrate, 5 g fat (1 g saturated), 34 mg cholesterol, 377 mg sodium.

Dry White Wine Choices

When a recipe calls for dry white wine, chablis, chardonnay, and sauvignon blanc are good choices. If you don't normally drink wine and want to use just a small amount at one time, look for single-serving size bottles, which often come in four-packs.

Vegetable Frittata

When you need a spur-of-the-moment meal, this egg dish saves the day. Serve it with sliced fresh tomatoes or cucumbers topped with a light vinaigrette and a hearty bread.

1 cup water
1 cup broccoli flowerets
½ cup finely chopped carrot
    Nonstick spray coating
¼ cup sliced green onions
¾ cup shredded reduced-fat cheddar
    or Swiss cheese (3 ounces)
2 8-ounce cartons refrigerated or
    frozen egg product, thawed
1 tablespoon snipped fresh basil or
    1 teaspoon dried basil, crushed
1 tablespoon Dijon-style mustard
¼ teaspoon pepper
    Tomato slices (optional)
    Fresh tarragon sprigs (optional)

In a medium saucepan combine water, broccoli, and carrot. Bring to boiling; reduce heat. Cover and simmer for 6 to 8 minutes or till vegetables are crisp-tender. Drain well.

Spray an unheated large nonstick skillet with nonstick coating. Spread broccoli, carrot, and green onions in the bottom of skillet. Sprinkle half of the cheese over vegetables. In a medium mixing bowl stir together egg product, basil, mustard, and pepper. Pour egg mixture into skillet over vegetables and cheese.

Cook over medium heat. As mixture sets, run a spatula around edge of skillet, lifting egg mixture so the uncooked portion flows underneath. Continue cooking and lifting the edge till egg mixture is almost set (the surface will be moist). Remove from heat.

Cover and let stand for 3 to 4 minutes or till top is set. To serve, cut into wedges. Sprinkle with the remaining cheese. If desired, garnish with tomato slices and tarragon sprigs. Makes 8 servings.

Nutrition information per serving: 101 calories, 11 g protein, 6 g carbohydrate, 3 g fat (1 g saturated), 6 mg cholesterol, 287 mg sodium.

Eggplant Parmigiana

Traditional eggplant parmigiana is loaded with fat and calories, but this version has only 212 calories and 6 grams of fat per serving. We kept the flavor by parboiling the eggplant and zucchini instead of frying them and by using reduced-fat cheeses.

1	medium eggplant (about 1 pound)
2	cups zucchini bias-sliced about ¼ inch thick
¼	teaspoon salt
1	cup low-fat ricotta cheese or cottage cheese, drained
1	15-ounce container refrigerated fat-free tomato-basil sauce or 2 cups light spaghetti sauce
1	small tomato, thinly sliced
½	cup shredded reduced-fat mozzarella cheese (2 ounces)
2	tablespoons grated Parmesan cheese

If desired, peel eggplant. Cut eggplant into ½-inch slices; halve each slice. In a large saucepan cook the eggplant, zucchini, and salt in a small amount of boiling water for 4 minutes. Drain vegetables; pat dry with paper towels.

Divide the eggplant and zucchini among 4 individual au gratin dishes or casseroles. Top with the ricotta or cottage cheese. Spoon the tomato-basil sauce or spaghetti sauce over cheese and top with the sliced tomato. Sprinkle with the mozzarella cheese and Parmesan cheese.

Bake, uncovered, in a 350° oven for 20 to 25 minutes or till heated through. Makes 4 servings.

Nutrition information per serving: 212 calories, 15 g protein, 27 g carbohydrate, 6 g fat (3 g saturated), 21 mg cholesterol, 560 mg sodium.

Eggplant—A Perennial Favorite

Dark purple, pear-shaped eggplant is popular with cooks for dishes such as Eggplant Parmigiana (above). There are several types of eggplant, available including western, white, Japanese, and small (baby) eggplant. When selecting an eggplant, look for a plump, glossy, heavy fruit. Don't buy one that has scarring, bruising, or a dull skin. The green stem cap should be fresh looking and free of mold. You can refrigerate an eggplant for up to 2 days before using.

Mexican-Style Scrambled Eggs

Extra-sharp cheddar cheese is more flavorful than its milder cousins—you don't have to use as much, which means fewer calories and less fat.

1 cup water
¼ cup thinly sliced green onions
¼ cup chopped red or green sweet pepper
1 8-ounce carton refrigerated or frozen egg product, thawed
¼ cup fat-free milk
⅛ teaspoon black pepper
4 7-inch flour tortillas
1 teaspoon margarine or butter
½ cup shredded reduced-fat cheddar cheese (2 ounces)
⅓ cup salsa

In a small saucepan combine water, green onions, and sweet pepper. Bring to boiling; reduce heat. Simmer, uncovered, for 5 to 7 minutes or till the vegetables are tender. Drain well. In a medium mixing bowl stir together the egg product, milk, and black pepper. Stir in drained vegetables.

Wrap tortillas in foil and bake in a 350° oven about 10 minutes or till warm. [Or, just before serving, microwave tortillas, covered, on 100% power (high) about 1 minute or till warm.]

Meanwhile, in a large skillet melt margarine or butter over medium heat. Pour in the egg mixture. Cook, without stirring, till mixture begins to set on bottom and around edge. Using a large spoon or spatula, lift and fold partially cooked eggs so uncooked portion flows underneath. Sprinkle with the cheddar cheese. Continue cooking for 2 to 3 minutes or till eggs are cooked through, but are still glossy and moist. (Be careful not to overcook the egg mixture.) Immediately remove from heat.

To serve, spoon the egg mixture down the centers of warm tortillas. Fold each tortilla in half or roll up. Top with the salsa. Makes 4 servings.

Nutrition information per serving: 230 calories, 15 g protein, 23 g carbohydrate, 8 g fat (2 g saturated), 11 mg cholesterol, 460 mg sodium.

Vegetable Lasagna

In a hurry? Substitute 2 cups of prepared spaghetti sauce for the Red Pepper Sauce in this recipe.

6 no-boil lasagna noodles or regular lasagna noodles
8 ounces zucchini and/or yellow summer squash, halved lengthwise and sliced
2 cups sliced fresh mushrooms
⅓ cup chopped onion
2 teaspoons olive oil
1 cup fat-free or low-fat ricotta cheese
¼ cup finely shredded Parmesan cheese
¼ teaspoon black pepper
Red Pepper Sauce
1 cup shredded part-skim mozzarella cheese (4 ounces)
1 medium tomato, seeded and chopped
Fresh oregano sprigs (optional)

Soak the no-boil lasagna noodles in warm water for 10 minutes. (Or, cook regular noodles according to package directions, except omit salt.) Drain.

Meanwhile, in a large skillet cook squash, mushrooms, and onion in hot oil about 6 minutes or till squash is tender, stirring occasionally. Drain well.

In a small bowl stir together ricotta cheese, Parmesan cheese, and black pepper. To assemble, place 3 lasagna noodles in a 2-quart square baking dish, trimming to fit as necessary. Top with ricotta mixture, half of the vegetable mixture, half of the Red Pepper Sauce, and half of the mozzarella cheese. Layer with remaining lasagna noodles, vegetables, and sauce.

Bake in a 375° oven for 30 minutes. Sprinkle with remaining mozzarella cheese and the tomato. Bake about 5 minutes more or till heated through. Let stand for 10 minutes before serving. If desired, garnish with oregano sprigs. Makes 6 servings.

Red Pepper Sauce: In a large skillet cook 3 cups chopped *red sweet pepper* and 4 whole cloves *garlic* in 1 tablespoon *olive oil* or *cooking oil* over medium heat for 20 minutes, stirring occasionally. (Or, use one 12-ounce jar *roasted red sweet peppers,* drained. Omit cooking step.) Place mixture in a blender container. Cover and blend till nearly smooth. Add ½ cup *water,* ¼ cup *tomato paste,* 2 tablespoons *red wine vinegar,* and 1 tablespoon snipped *fresh oregano* or ½ teaspoon *dried oregano,* crushed. Cover and blend just till nearly smooth. Return to skillet; heat through. Makes 2 cups.

Nutrition information per serving: 249 calories, 17 g protein, 28 g carbohydrate, 9 g fat (3 g saturated), 18 mg cholesterol, 292 mg sodium.

INDEX

A-E

Apricot-Stuffed Grilled Turkey Breast 22
Beans
     Grilled Tuna with Tuscan Beans 32
     Turkey Taco Salad 29
Beef
     Bolognese Meat Sauce with Pasta 13
     Garlic-Sage-Marinated Beef Pot Roast 6
     Marinated Steak Fajitas 8
     Midwest Swiss Steak with Tomato Gravy 9
     Peppered Steak with Mushroom Gravy 11
     Spaghetti with Italian Meatballs 12
Bolognese Meat Sauce with Pasta 13
Casseroles
     Chicken and Biscuit Pie .30
     Eggplant Parmigiana 42
     Vegetable Lasagna 45
Chicken
     Chicken and Biscuit Pie .30
     Easy Orange-Glazed Chicken 26
     Fruity Chicken Salad Sandwiches 26
     Grilled Chicken and Vegetable Kabobs 24
     Hot 'n' Sweet Barbecued Chicken 28
     Jamaican Jerk Chicken 25
     Roasted Peppers and Chicken Skillet 23
     Turkey Taco Salad 29
Clam Sauce with Spaghetti, White 40
Easy Orange-Glazed Chicken .26
Eggplant Parmigiana 42
Eggs
     Mexican-Style Scrambled Eggs 43
     Vegetable Frittata 41

F-O

Fajitas, Marinated Steak 8
Fish
     Fish Fillets with Red Pepper Sauce 33
     Grilled Tuna with Tuscan Beans 32
     Herbed Halibut 36
     Salmon with Wilted Greens 35
     Seafood Jambalaya 37
     Sweet and Sour Mahimahi 36
Fruity Chicken Salad Sandwiches 26
Garlic-Sage-Marinated Beef Pot Roast 6
Green Onion Biscuits 30
Grilled Recipes
     Apricot-Stuffed Grilled Turkey Breast 22
     Grilled Apricot-Stuffed Pork Chops 14
     Grilled Chicken and Vegetable Kabobs 24
     Grilled Tuna with Tuscan Beans 32
     Hot 'n' Sweet Barbecued Chicken 28
     Jamaican Jerk Chicken 25
     Salmon with Wilted Greens 35
Herbed Halibut 36
Homemade Cajun Seasoning .37

Hot 'n' Sweet Barbecued Chicken 28
Italian Pot Roast 16
Jalapeño Shrimp and Pasta 38
Jamaican Jerk Chicken 25
Kabobs
     Grilled Chicken and Vegetable Kabobs 24
     Jamaican Jerk Chicken 25
Lamb Chops and Peppers 21
Marinated Steak Fajitas 8
Mexican-Style Scrambled Eggs 43
Midwest Swiss Steak with Tomato Gravy 9
Mustard-Orange Pork Tenderloin 17

P-Z

Pasta
     Bolognese Meat Sauce with Pasta 13
     Jalapeño Shrimp and Pasta 38
     Spaghetti with Italian Meatballs 12
     Vegetable Lasagna 45
     White Clam Sauce with Spaghetti 40
Peppered Pork & Apricot Salad 19
Peppered Steak with Mushroom Gravy 11
Pork
     Grilled Apricot-Stuffed Pork Chops 14
     Italian Pot Roast 16
     Mustard-Orange Pork Tenderloin 17
     Peppered Pork & Apricot Salad 19
     Spicy Pork Chops 20
Red Pepper Sauce 45
Roasted Peppers and Chicken Skillet 23
Salad, Peppered Pork & Apricot 19
Salad, Turkey Taco 29
Salmon with Wilted Greens 35
Sandwiches, Fruity Chicken Salad 26
Seafood Jambalaya 37
Shrimp
     Jalapeño Shrimp and Pasta 38
     Seafood Jambalaya 37
Spaghetti with Italian Meatballs 12
Spicy Pork Chops 20
Sweet and Sour Mahimahi 36
Tomatoes
     Bolognese Meat Sauce with Pasta 13
     Grilled Tuna with Tuscan Beans 32
     Jalapeño Shrimp and Pasta 38
     Midwest Swiss Steak with Tomato Gravy 9
     Roasted Peppers and Chicken Skillet 23
     Seafood Jambalaya 37
     Spaghetti with Italian Meatballs 12
     Turkey Taco Salad 29
Turkey
     Apricot-Stuffed Grilled Turkey Breast 22
     Turkey Taco Salad 29
Vegetable Frittata 41
Vegetable Lasagna 45
White Clam Sauce with Spaghetti 40